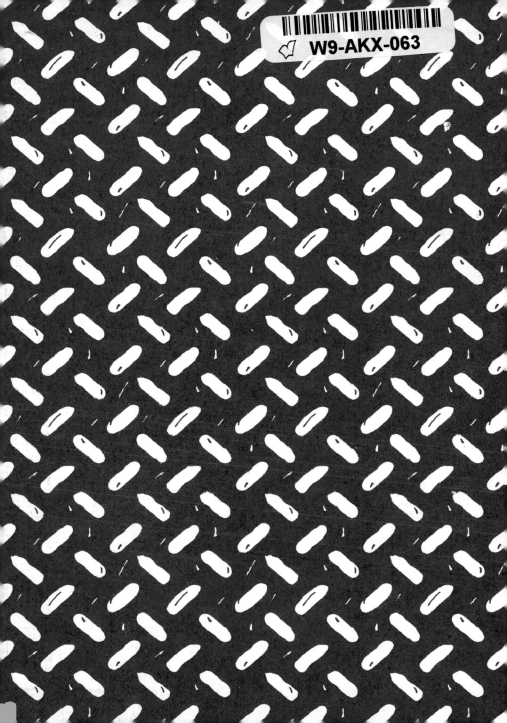

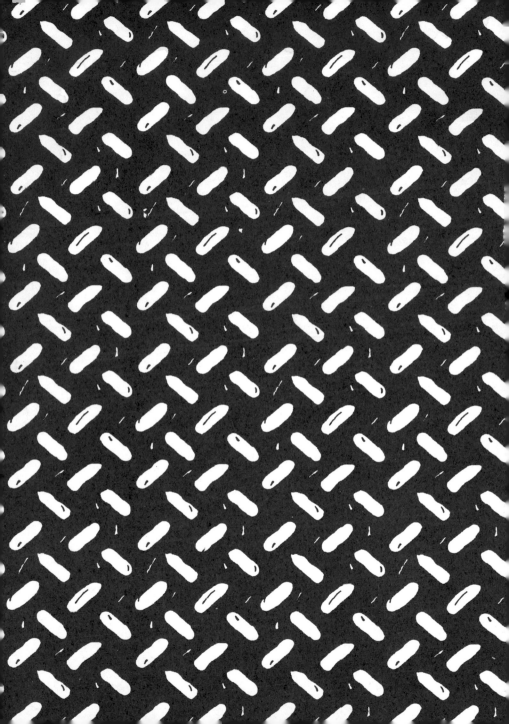

THE
LITTLE
GRAIN
COOKBOOK

THE
LITTLE
GRAIN
COOKBOOK

BY PATRICIA STAPLEY

ILLUSTRATIONS BY JENNIE OPPENHEIMER

CROWN PUBLISHERS, INC.
NEW YORK

Published by Crown Publishers, Inc., 201 East 50th Street, New York, New York 10022.
Member of the Crown Publishing Group.

CROWN is a trademark of Crown Publishers, Inc.

Manufactured in Hong Kong

Library of Congress Cataloging-in-Publication Data
Stapley, Patricia,
The little grain cookbook / by Patricia Stapley; illustrations by Jennie Oppenheimer.—1st ed.
p.   cm.
Includes index.
1. Cookery (Cereals)   2. Grain.   I. Title.
TX809.S72   1991
641.6'31— dc20   91-11912
CIP

ISBN 0-517-58356-9

10 9   8   7   6   5   4   3   2   1

FIRST EDITION

F 🪰 Y
PRODUCTIONS

CONTENTS

INTRODUCTION

Wholesome, delicious, and health-giving grains have nourished the world for thousands of years. Grains present a limitless source of low-cost, nutrition-rich eating pleasure and will undoubtedly become an increasingly important food in the future. Their outstanding flavors and amazing versatility are inspiring chefs and restaurateurs to create exciting new cuisines for all of us to enjoy.

Grains are the ripened seeds or fruits of grasses. When grains are processed simply — that is, left unbleached and left whole or ground up without any parts removed — they are high in fiber, low in fat, and an excellent source of protein.

The many grains celebrated in *The Little Grain Cookbook* can be found, neatly packaged, at your local supermarket. You can rest assured that they are carefully cleaned before they are packaged. If organically grown produce is important to you, you'll want to shop for your grains at a health food store. The selection will be larger, and often you will have the option of buying just as much or as little as you wish.

Grains such as barley, bulgur (or bulghur) wheat, cornmeal, grits and masa harina (dried hominy), quinoa, rolled oats, and rice will keep for as long as a year sealed in tightly covered containers and stored in a cool, dry place. Unhulled grains with the germ still intact, such as wheat berries, whole oats, and wild rice, have a higher oil content than refined grains. Store these whole grains in the refrigerator or freezer to preserve their freshness.

All grains use the same basic cooking method. "The Little Grain Cooking Guide," below, will help you determine the amount of liquid necessary for the various grains you will be using, the final yield, and the approximate cooking time. About half of the recipes call for already cooked grains; the rest call for uncooked grains and feature special cooking instructions.

Grains are really very easy to cook: you simply add the raw grain to boiling liquid. For the liquid, I generally use water, but you can use chicken, meat, or vegetable stock to produce a more flavorful cooked grain. After you add the

THE LITTLE GRAIN COOKING GUIDE

DRY GRAIN (1/2 Cup)	LIQUID (Cups)	YIELD (Cups)	APPROXIMATE COOKING TIME
Barley	1 1/3	1 3/4	40 minutes
Bulgur	1	1 1/2	20 minutes
Cornmeal	1 1/2	1 1/2	5 minutes
Couscous (Quick)	2/3	1	5 minutes
Grits	2	2	10 minutes
Quinoa	1	1 3/4	15 minutes
Rolled oats	1	1	5 minutes
Wheat berries	1 3/4	1 1/3	90 minutes
Whole oats	1	1 1/4	30 minutes
White rice	1	1 1/2	20 minutes
Wild rice	1 1/4	2 1/3	55 minutes

grain to the liquid, stir once, let the liquid return to a boil, reduce the heat to low, cover the pot, and let the grain cook slowly until the liquid has been absorbed. Or, with some grains, turn off the heat and let the grain stand in a covered pot until the liquid is absorbed. This can take anywhere from five minutes for finely ground grains to one and a half hours for whole, unhulled grains.

When precooking grains, I like to use a bit less liquid than is called for. Then, if the grain has absorbed it all and still is not quite done, I add a little more liquid, re-cover, and continue to cook. A grain cooked to perfection has a lively, chewy texture. Overcooked grains or grains cooked in too much water collapse and become sticky and pasty. Remember, when cooking grains, less is more. You are merely swelling them and making them tender.

At the end of each recipe is a listing of the amounts of fiber, cholesterol, fat, and calories in each serving. A few of the recipes also have a "Lean Grain Tip" that will help you modify it for diets restricted in saturated fat or cholesterol, while still leaving your main course wonderfully delicious.

Treat your guests to inspired and healthful meals — a rustic Italian polenta, an exotic Egyptian couscous, tamales from the Amazon rain forest, a delightful grain soufflé. The recipes in *The Little Grain Cookbook* will allow you to experience a fresh attitude toward ingredients and new culinary techniques that are showing up on the finest tables in the world.

San Antonio Five-Alarm Chili and Fiery Corn Sticks, Damn!

Earn stars and stripes for serving this tasty sensation, a Fourth of July natural. The fireworks won't hold a candle to the stars in your guests' eyes as they sit down to enjoy the flavor-packed San Antonio Five-Alarm Chili and Fiery Corn Sticks. It's a hot and spicy mouthful, so be prepared to cool your guests down with a chilled watermelon fruit salad. If the weather's right, you'll want to eat this meal out of doors just as the sun sets and the sky show begins.

Makes Six to Eight Servings

FIVE-ALARM CHILI

> 2 tablespoons olive oil
> 1 large onion, finely chopped
> 2 garlic cloves, minced
> 2 medium zucchini, finely chopped
> 1 medium green bell pepper, cored, seeded, and
>   finely chopped
> 2 cups cooked pinto beans, drained
> 4 medium plum tomatoes, chopped
> 1 35-ounce can Italian plum tomatoes, undrained
> 1 cup chicken, beef, or vegetable stock

11

1 cup corn kernels
1 cup uncooked barley
2 serrano chilies, cored, seeded, and diced
1/4 cup chopped cilantro (fresh coriander)
1 teaspoon ground cumin
1/2 teaspoon dried oregano
1/2 teaspoon cayenne pepper
1/2 teaspoon salt
1/2 teaspoon freshly ground black pepper
2 medium avocados, peeled and cubed, for garnish

FIERY CORN STICKS

3 cups white cornmeal
1 cup all-purpose flour
4 teaspoons baking powder
2 teaspoons baking soda
2 teaspoons salt
2 tablespoons sugar
4 eggs
3 cups buttermilk
6 tablespoons unsalted butter
1 jalapeño pepper, cored, seeded, and diced
1/3 cup diced sharp cheddar cheese

Heat the oil in a large heavy pan over medium-low heat. Sauté the onion and garlic until soft, about three minutes. Add the zucchini and the green pepper and sauté for three minutes more. Add the beans, chopped and canned tomatoes and tomato liquid, stock, corn, barley, chilies, and cilantro. Stir to combine thoroughly. Sprinkle in the cumin, oregano, cayenne, salt, and black pepper. Simmer uncovered for thirty minutes, stirring frequently.

Meanwhile, prepare the Fiery Corn Sticks. Preheat the oven to 425 degrees.

Sift the cornmeal, flour, baking powder, baking soda, salt, and sugar into a large bowl. Mix well to combine.

Beat the eggs in a medium-sized bowl. Add the buttermilk and beat well.

In a small saucepan, melt the butter over medium-low heat. Vigorously beat it into the egg-milk mixture. Add to the dry ingredients and stir thoroughly. Add the jalapeño and cheese, and fold gently to mix through the batter.

Butter a cast iron corn stick pan. Pour the batter into the pan, filling each mold three quarters full. There is enough batter for two batches, or twenty-four cornsticks. Bake until the tops are lightly browned, fifteen to twenty minutes.

Ladle the steaming chili into shallow bowls centered on dinner plates. Garnish each bowl with cubes of buttery avocado. Arrange four cornsticks on each plate, pointing north, south, east, and west. Serve at once.

Lean Grain Tip: Garnish the chili with plain popped corn instead of avocado. In the corn sticks, replace the buttermilk with low-fat milk. Use egg substitute instead of whole eggs, and margarine instead of butter.

Each Lean Grain serving contains:

- FIBER: 2.2 GRAMS • CHOLESTEROL: 3.8 MILLIGRAMS
- FAT: 12.9 GRAMS • CALORIES: 507

Medallions of
Faux Veau
on Glossed Spinach

Grits are coarsely ground cornmeal, with a heartwarming, nutty flavor. In Medallions of Faux Veau, the cooked grits are formed into veal-chop-sized morsels that will delight your dinner companions' tastes for inventive cuisine. This exciting entree captures the simple and delicious flavors that are uniquely Provençal. Serve this chic main course with a warmed mussel and arugula salad and a rich red Burgundy. Finish with a caramelized pear tart.

Makes Four Servings

5 cups water
1 teaspoon salt
1 cup uncooked grits
2 tablespoons coarsely chopped rosemary leaves
1/2 teaspoon cracked black pepper
6 tablespoons olive oil
15 garlic cloves, peeled and thinly sliced
4 1/2 tablespoons balsamic vinegar
2 pounds fresh spinach, trimmed and washed

In a large heavy-bottomed saucepan, bring the water and salt to a boil over high heat. Reduce the heat and add the grits, whisking them into the barely simmering water so that the grains separate.

Stirring occasionally, cook the grits, uncovered, for about ten minutes, until smooth and thick. Pour the grits onto a large baking sheet to make a layer about three quarters of an inch thick. Cover with wax paper and set aside. After the grits have cooled to room temperature, refrigerate for at least one hour to harden.

Remove the grits from the refrigerator and cut creatively with a knife into kidney-shaped medallions about three to four inches across, wasting as little of the grits as possible. You should end up with eight medallions.

Scatter the rosemary and cracked pepper on a flat plate. Press the medallions into the chopped leaves to impregnate both sides with the flavorful herb.

Preheat the oven to 225 degrees.

In a large heavy skillet, heat two tablespoons of oil over medium heat. Sauté the medallions, as many as will fit, for about four minutes, turning once as they brown. They will be golden brown on both sides when done. Transfer the medallions to a baking dish and put them in the oven to keep warm.

In the same skillet, combine the garlic and another two tablespoons of olive oil. Cover the skillet and cook over very low heat until the garlic is tender, about five minutes. Uncover the skillet, increase the heat to moderate, and cook for another minute or two, until the garlic begins to brown lightly. Stir in the vinegar and simmer for one minute more, stirring and scraping the bottom of the pan. Turn off the heat, cover the pan, and set the gravy aside.

Meanwhile, dry the spinach thoroughly in a salad

spinner or pat dry with paper towels. Heat the remaining oil in another large skillet over medium-low heat. Add the spinach and cook, stirring and tossing occasionally, until tender and well coated, three to four minutes. Do not overcook the spinach.

Arrange the spinach on a warmed serving platter to form a lovely green bed. Remove the medallions from the oven and place them in a single layer on top of the spinach. Drizzle a bit of the gravy over each medallion. Bring the platter to the table and serve at once.

Each serving contains:
• FIBER: 1.7 GRAMS • CHOLESTEROL: 0 MILLIGRAMS
• FAT: 18 GRAMS • CALORIES: 356

Café Mykonos
Barley, Feta, and Olive
Odyssey

Here is a dish inspired by idyllic holidays on the whitewashed island of Mykonos. The natural earthy flavor of barley, tangy marinated onions, and the pungent combination of feta and kalamata olives are a divine variation on the immortal Greek salad. It's perfectly portable — you can spread a white cloth under a shade tree and serve your picnic repast on lively Grecian-style pottery. Whiling away the better part of the day with a chilled bottle of wood-cured retsina, you'll come to believe you're actually basking on a windswept hill overlooking the azure Aegean.

Makes Four Servings

1/3 cup virgin olive oil
1/4 cup balsamic vinegar
3 tablespoons dried oregano
2 garlic cloves, minced
salt and freshly ground black pepper to taste
1 large red onion
2 cucumbers (peeled if waxed)
2 medium ripe tomatoes
1 red bell pepper, cored and seeded

1 green bell pepper, cored and seeded
1 cup cooked barley, cooled
8 ounces feta cheese, coarsely crumbled
20 kalamata olives (pitted if desired)

In a small nonmetallic bowl, whisk together the oil, vinegar, oregano, garlic, and salt and pepper to make an oregano vinaigrette.

Cut the onion into twenty paper-thin slices. Put the slices in a medium-sized glass or ceramic bowl. Drizzle one tablespoon of the vinaigrette over the onions and gently toss to coat. Set aside to marinate for about fifteen minutes.

In the meantime, cut the cucumbers into round slices one eighth inch thick. Cut the tomatoes into quarter-inch slices. Slice the red and green peppers into rings one quarter inch thick.

Compose the Café Mykonos Barley, Feta, and Olive Odyssey into a pretty pattern on four large salad plates. Start with a layer of cucumbers, then a layer of marinated onion, then a layer of tomatoes, and then alternating layers of red and green peppers. Place a delicate mound of the barley in the center of each salad, and top with the feta and olives.

Dress each salad with the remaining vinaigrette, and serve immediately.

Lean Grain Tip: Omit the feta cheese.

Each Lean Grain serving contains:

- FIBER: 2.5 GRAMS • CHOLESTEROL: 0 MILLIGRAMS
- FAT: 25 GRAMS • CALORIES: 349

Wild Rice,
Wild Mushroom, and
Wild Turkey Pottage

After a brisk outing in the fall countryside, one and all will look forward to a bowl of this wild-at-heart soup. You can present the best of the Oktoberfest harvest season with the addition of a rustic spinach and pancetta salad, a bottle of the year's first Beaujolais nouveau, and a crisp apple tart.

Makes Four Servings

1 cup uncooked wild rice
2 quarts chicken stock
1 pound fresh wild mushrooms (morels, chanterelles,
    porcini, or shiitake, or a mixture if you wish)
2 tablespoons unsalted butter
2 medium shallots, minced
2 tablespoons fresh lemon juice
1/2 cup heavy cream
1 tablespoon minced fresh thyme
2 tablespoons Wild Turkey bourbon, or to taste
salt and freshly ground black pepper to taste
4 fresh thyme sprigs, for garnish

In a strainer, rinse the wild rice thoroughly under cold running water. Drain.

In a medium-sized saucepan, bring the stock to a boil over high heat. Add the wild rice and bring the stock back to a boil. Reduce the heat to low, cover the pan, and simmer the wild rice until soft, about one and a half hours.

When the wild rice is done, transfer just a portion — one and a half cups — to a food processor or blender, and purée until smooth. Add the purée to the saucepan of soup and stir. Let the soup continue to simmer slowly while you prepare the other ingredients.

Clean the mushrooms with a damp cloth. Trim off any tough stems and finely chop the mushrooms.

Melt the butter in a skillet over medium heat. Add the shallots and sauté until soft but not browned, about two minutes. Add the mushrooms and lemon juice. Sauté until the liquid has evaporated, about five minutes.

Stir the sautéed mushrooms and shallots into the soup. Turn the heat up to medium. Stir in the cream and minced thyme. Stirring frequently, bring the soup to a boil. Reduce the heat to low and simmer, uncovered, for about fifteen minutes, or until it becomes thick and creamy.

Remove from the heat and add the bourbon. Season with salt and pepper.

Carry out your fall theme by placing a single red or gold autumn leaf beneath each clear glass soup bowl. Serve your tureen of steaming pottage with a garnish of thyme sprigs.

Lean Grain Tip: Omit the cream. Replace the butter with margarine.

Each Lean Grain serving contains:

- FIBER: .6 GRAMS • CHOLESTEROL: 0 MILLIGRAMS
- FAT: 9.7 GRAMS • CALORIES: 365

Stuffed Onion Marrakech with Bulgur, Mint, and Pomegranate

Take a bite and savor the aromatic and mouth-watering flavors of elegant Moroccan cuisine. Stuffed Onion Marrakech with Bulgur, Mint, and Pomegranate — an exotic entree by anyone's standards — will transport your friends to the shores of North Africa. Seat your guests on cushions around a low table scattered here and there with fresh rose petals. Fill little glass dishes with lemon-spiked yogurt, arrange plates of fresh roasted almonds and sun-dried apricots within everyone's reach, and tantalize their taste buds with a pot of enchanting *thé de menthe.*

Makes Six Servings

6 large onions
1 cup uncooked bulgur wheat
1 ripe tomato, peeled and chopped
4 tablespoons finely chopped fresh mint leaves
1/2 cup pomegranate seeds, plus 2 tablespoons for
    garnish
1/4 cup pine nuts
1 teaspoon ground cinnamon
salt and freshly ground black pepper to taste

1 tablespoon butter
1 tablespoon all-purpose flour
3 tablespoons tomato paste
1 cup water
1/2 lemon

Bring a large pot of water to a boil.

Peel the onions, leaving the tops and root ends on for the moment. Plunge them into the boiling water. (Be sure you've boiled enough water to cover them.) Cook the onions until they are fairly tender, ten to fifteen minutes. Drain the onions and let them cool. When they are cool enough to handle, cut a thin slice off the root end and carefully scoop out the center of each onion and discard, leaving shells three or four layers thick and the top of the onion intact. Set them aside.

Put the bulgur, tomato, mint, the half cup of pomegranate seeds, pine nuts, cinnamon, and salt and pepper in a medium bowl. Mix thoroughly and set aside.

Melt the butter in a small pan over medium heat. Blend in the flour and cook for one minute. Add the tomato paste and stir well. Gradually add the water, stirring constantly. Season with salt and pepper. Remove the tomato sauce from the heat.

Stuff the onion shells three quarters full with the bulgur mixture. The filling will expand as it cooks.

Place the onions side by side, open end up, in a large saucepan. Pour in enough tomato sauce to cover the onions halfway up. Cover the saucepan and simmer the onions gently over low heat for forty-five minutes. When the onions are done they will be tender but still whole.

Pool a bit of the remaining tomato sauce on each plate and place an Onion Marrakech in the center. Garnish the top of each steaming stuffed onion with the remaining pomegranate seeds and squeeze a few drops of lemon juice on top. Be sure to serve the perfect accompaniment — a basket of warm, crusty pita bread to help you scoop up every savory mouthful.

Lean Grain Tip: Use margarine in place of butter.

Each Lean Grain serving contains:
- FIBER: 2.2 GRAMS • CHOLESTEROL: 0 MILLIGRAMS
- FAT: 7.5 GRAMS • CALORIES: 274

Top Hat Grain Soufflé with Dancing Ginger Sauce

As brilliantly paired as Fred Astaire and Ginger Rogers, Top Hat Grain Soufflé with Dancing Ginger Sauce is the ideal culinary centerpiece for your next black tie (and tails) dinner party. Serve this dazzling creation with lobster bisque, a silver tray array of grilled vegetables drizzled with lemon and garnished with basil, and sparkling flutes of Roederer Cristal. Your guests will soon be cheek to cheek, dancing the Continental.

Makes Six Servings

TOP HAT SOUFFLÉ

> 1 tablespoon unsalted butter
> 2 tablespoons olive oil
> 1 large shallot, minced
> 1/3 cup minced celery leaves
> 2 scallions, minced, tops included
> 1/2 teaspoon ground ginger
> 1/2 teaspoon curry powder
> 1/2 teaspoon dried thyme
> 1/2 teaspoon dried red pepper flakes
> 1/2 teaspoon salt

freshly ground black pepper to taste
3 tablespoons barley flour
2/3 cup oat bran
2 cups milk
1 egg yolk
5 egg whites
1/2 cup shredded garlic Jack cheese

DANCING GINGER SAUCE

2 tablespoons unsalted butter
3 tablespoons all-purpose flour
1 cup hot chicken stock
1 tablespoon minced fresh ginger
1/2 teaspoon grated fresh ginger
1/2 teaspoon minced chives
1 tablespoon grated or minced lime zest
1/4 cup heavy cream
1 teaspoon lime juice

Preheat the oven to 400 degrees. Butter a two-quart soufflé dish and set it aside.

In a medium saucepan, heat the oil at a low temperature. Add the shallot, celery leaves, scallions, ginger, curry powder, thyme, red pepper, salt, and black pepper. Sauté for three minutes. Stir in the barley flour until smooth. Cook for one minute. Remove the saucepan from the heat and set it aside to cool.

Put the oat bran in another medium-sized saucepan. Pour the milk over it and heat the mixture slowly, stirring often, until it comes to a boil. Reduce the heat and simmer. After about three minutes it will become thick and smooth.

Remove from the heat and whisk in the egg yolk. Stir in the cooled barley flour mixture.

Beat the egg whites in a bowl until they stiffen to form peaks. Fold one quarter of the whites into the bran–barley flour mixture. Quickly and gently fold in the remaining whites. Fold in the cheese, being careful not to deflate the volume of the batter. Spoon it swiftly and softly into the soufflé dish, and place it on a shelf in the bottom third of the oven. Bake the soufflé about thirty minutes.

Meanwhile, start the Dancing Ginger Sauce by melting the butter in a heavy-bottomed saucepan. Stir in the flour and blend over moderate heat until smooth. Continue to cook, stirring constantly, for two minutes. Add the stock and continue stirring as the mixture thickens. Bring to a boil, lower the heat, and simmer for two minutes. Add the ginger, chives, and lime zest. Simmer for two minutes longer. Stir in the cream and lime juice. Cook for one more minute. Transfer the sauce to a silver sauceboat that can sit elegantly beside the Top Hat Soufflé.

Remove the soufflé from the oven when it is golden and puffed but still moist inside. Bring it to the table immediately. Scoop out a melt-in-your-mouth portion for each of your guests, and let them help themselves to the remarkable Dancing Ginger Sauce.

Lean Grain Tip: In the soufflé, substitute margarine for the butter and low-fat milk for whole milk. In the ginger sauce, substitute margarine for the butter.

Each Lean Grain serving contains:

- FIBER: 3 GRAMS • CHOLESTEROL: 84.5 MILLIGRAMS
- FAT: 23.8 GRAMS • CALORIES: 374

Rain Forest Tamales with Mango Salsa

Why not throw a *tamalada,* or tamale party, to celebrate the bounty of the rain forest? Make it a true fiesta by decorating your table with colorful South American flair. Then bring on the Rain Forest Tamales piled high on a platter, accompanied by Mango Salsa, sour cream, and wedges of lemon. Serve pitchers of tropical fruit sangrias, and sliced fresh pineapple for dessert. Your guests — and friends of the rain forest — will savor some of the earth's most endangered treasures.

Makes Twenty Tamales (Serves Eight to Ten)

6 or 7 unhusked ears of corn (or substitute 3 cups of corn kernels and a bag of dried corn husks, available at specialty food stores)
1/2 cup water
1 teaspoon salt
2 cups masa harina
1 tablespoon sugar
1 cup vegetable shortening
1 teaspoon baking powder
5 or 6 Anaheim chilies (or substitute canned green chilies)

3/4 cup uncooked quinoa
20 Brazil nuts, shelled
1/2 pound Monterey Jack cheese
Mango Salsa (recipe follows)

If you are using fresh corn, cut through each cob at its thickest point, just above the stem. Discard the stems. Very carefully, so that they do not tear, unwrap the husks from the ears. Rinse the husks, and place them on paper towels to dry while you prepare the filling.

If you use dried corn husks, select about twenty-five of the largest. The husks need to be about seven inches long by three inches wide, so if you don't have a sufficient quantity this big, make up the difference by selecting two smaller husks for every large one. Soak the husks in a large bowl of warm water until they become pliable, about five minutes. Rinse, drain, and leave to dry on paper towels.

Remove the silk from the fresh corn and cut the kernels off the cobs. Put the corn kernels and water in a food processor or blender. Process to a medium-coarse purée. Add the salt, masa harina, sugar, shortening, and baking powder. Process for about a minute, until the dough is light and thoroughly blended.

If you are using fresh chilies, preheat the broiler. Place the chilies under the broiler and turn them to char on all sides. When the skins are thoroughly charred and the flesh is softened, remove the chilies and put them in a plastic bag. Close the bag and let the chilies sweat for ten minutes. Remove them from the bag, peel them, cut them in half, and discard their seeds and stems. Chop the chilies finely. If you use canned chilies, drain, seed, and chop finely. Place the chilies in a medium-sized glass bowl and set aside.

Season a heavy-bottomed skillet with salt and set over medium heat. Add the quinoa and toast it for two minutes, stirring frequently to prevent burning. Remove the grain from the skillet and add it to the chilies. Mix well and set aside.

Return the skillet to the heat and add the Brazil nuts. Toast for two minutes, stirring frequently. Remove the nuts and set them aside in a small bowl.

Cut the cheese into sticks about three inches long by a quarter inch wide and deep. Set aside.

To make the tamale ties, select three corn husks at least four inches long. Starting at the narrow end, rip each husk vertically into strips about one eighth inch wide. Set aside.

Select one of the larger corn husks. Place two table-spoons of the dough in the middle of the husk. Spread the dough to form a thin rectangle about three inches long. Leave enough husk empty to create an envelope — about two inches at the top and an inch on either side.

Place a tablespoon of the quinoa-chili mixture in the center of the dough. Top with a strip of cheese and place a Brazil nut in the middle.

Fold the sides of the husk over the filling so that they overlap, then fold up the bottom to make an open-ended parcel. Take one of the corn husk strips and tie it in a knot around the folded-up tamal, to hold it. The parcel should not be tied too tightly, as the filling will expand as it cooks. Repeat to make the rest of the tamales. If you run out of large husks, overlap two smaller husks.

Prepare a steamer. Set the tamales in the steamer, layered on the top of each other, and steam for one and a half hours. You can stack them on a platter and serve them immediately. Your guests will unwrap the the tamales from the husks and douse them with the Mango Salsa.

The cooked and wrapped tamales can also be refrigerated or frozen, stored about five to a bag. To reheat them straight from the refrigerator or freezer, preheat the oven to 350 degrees, wrap the tamales individually in foil, and heat through for about thirty minutes. If you prefer to microwave, reheat refrigerated tamales for about two minutes, frozen tamales for about five minutes.

Each serving contains:

- FIBER: 2.3 GRAMS • CHOLESTEROL: 12 MILLIGRAMS
- FAT: 33 GRAMS • CALORIES: 548

Mango Salsa

While the tamales are steaming, prepare the Mango Salsa.

Makes 2 Cups

2 ripe mangoes, cut into medium dice
juice of 1/2 lemon
4 to 6 jalapeño or serrano chilies, cored, seeded, and
    finely chopped
1/4 cup chopped cilantro (fresh coriander)
4 scallions chopped, tops included
1/2 teaspoon salt

Combine all the ingredients in a glass bowl and refrigerate until ready to serve.

Blue Plate Special: Mom's Spa Meat Loaf

Warm the heart of Everymom and serve up a healthy dish of the premiere comfort food — Mom's Spa Meat Loaf. This spa loaf is made with a mixture of light and lively grains and vegetables that taste terrific. The Blue Plate Special — featured in diners all across America — will become a truly authentic offering served with a slice of cherry pie and a cup of freshly brewed java. Eat up — make your mom proud!

Makes Six Servings

1 1/2 cups cooked and drained pinto beans
2 cups cooked pearl barley, cooled
1 1/2 teaspoons freshly ground black pepper
1 1/2 teaspoons paprika
1 1/4 teaspoon ground cumin
1/2 teaspoon thyme
2 teaspoons olive oil
2 medium onions, coarsely chopped
1 red bell pepper, cored, seeded, and coarsely
    chopped
1 small jalapeño pepper, seeded and minced
1 tablespoon minced garlic

1 1/2 tablespoons Worcestershire sauce
1/2 cup tomato purée
2 teaspoons vinegar
1/2 cup beef, chicken, or vegetable stock
1 cup uncooked rolled oats
3 egg whites
lemon wedges and parsley sprigs, for garnish

Put the pinto beans and barley in a food processor or blender. Pulse until partially blended, letting some of the beans remain whole. Transfer to a large glass mixing bowl.

In a small bowl, combine the black pepper, paprika, cumin, and thyme.

In a large heavy-bottomed skillet, heat the oil over moderate heat. Add the onions, bell pepper, jalapeño, garlic, Worcestershire sauce, and combined spices. Sauté, stirring once or twice, until the vegetables start to stick to the bottom of the skillet, about six minutes. Stir in the tomato purée, vinegar, and stock. Continue to cook, stirring occasionally, until the mixture is quite thick, about twelve minutes. Reduce the heat if necessary to prevent scorching. Remove the saucepan from the heat and set aside to cool.

Line a nine-by-thirteen-inch baking dish with foil.

Preheat the oven to 350 degrees.

Stir the sautéed vegetables into the beans and barley. Add the rolled oats and mix well. Fold in the egg whites. Mix until all the ingredients are completely combined (the way your mom always told you to — with your clean hands!).

Mound the mixture in the center of the baking dish. Shape it into a loaf about ten inches long by five inches wide. Bake the loaf for thirty minutes, until browned. Before serving, let the loaf cool for at least five minutes.

Assemble each Blue Plate Special in the kitchen on everyday dinnerware — a slab of spa loaf, a heaping portion of fluffy mashed potatoes, a big spoonful of green beans, and a lemon wedge and sprig of parsley for garnish.

Each serving contains:

- FIBER: 1.7 GRAMS • CHOLESTEROL: 0 MILLIGRAMS
- FAT: 2 GRAMS • CALORIES: 304

The Roman Risotto of Mrs. Stone with Trout and Grilled Onion

Take your guests on a Roman holiday with the rich flavors of The Roman Risotto of Mrs. Stone with Trout and Grilled Onion. The irresistible combination of creamy rice, wood-smoked trout, and sweet red onion will conquer even the most jaded appetite — especially when accompanied by a salad of arugula, Gorgonzola, and sliced apples. Lift a glass of mellow Verdicchio to toast this meal fit for an emperor, and finish late in the night with cordials of sambuca with floating coffee beans.

Makes Four Servings

1 smoked trout
1 large red onion
3 tablespoons plus 1 teaspoon olive oil
5 cups chicken or vegetable stock
1 large shallot, finely chopped
1 1/2 cups uncooked Arborio or Cristallo rice
1/2 cup freshly grated Parmesan cheese

Skin and flake the trout. Set aside.

Preheat the broiler. Peel the onion and slice it into quarter-inch-thick rounds. Brush the onion slices lightly on both sides with the teaspoon of oil. Place the onions on a baking sheet and grill them under the broiler until they are well browned but not blackened. Turn them over and brown on the other side. Remove the onions from the broiler and let them cool slightly. Separate them into rings and set aside.

In a medium saucepan, heat the chicken stock to a slow, steady simmer.

In a heavy-bottomed skillet, heat the three tablespoons of oil. Add the shallot and sauté over medium-high heat until it becomes translucent. Add the rice, and agitate until each grain is well coated with oil. Lightly sauté for about two minutes.

Add half a cup of the simmering stock to the rice and stir very gently for three or four minutes, until the rice has absorbed the liquid. Repeat this process, continuing to add the warm stock by half cups to the skillet of rice. Cook, stirring constantly, until all of the stock has been incorporated and the risotto is creamy and just tender, about thirty minutes.

Remove the skillet from the heat. Add the Parmesan cheese and fold in thoroughly to melt.

Spread the steaming risotto on a warmed platter and decorate the top with morsels of smoked trout and rings of grilled onion. Serve piping hot.

Lean Grain Tip: Omit the Parmesan cheese.

Each Lean Grain serving contains:

- FIBER: .7 GRAMS • CHOLESTEROL: 0 MILLIGRAMS
- FAT: 16 GRAMS • CALORIES: 269

Hot and Cold Szechuan Grain Nut Salad

The fire of the dragon's tongue and the cold bite of winter snows mingle in this sophisticated salad. Every forkful offers a unique flavor or texture. The wheat berries make a deliciously nutty change from that other little Chinese grain, rice. Your friends will enjoy serving the Szechuan Grain Nut Salad to themselves from a richly patterned chinoiserie bowl. Delicate porcelain cups of Lapsang Souchong tea and sweet mandarin orange sections arranged on a bed of ice are an elegant solution to impromptu guests on a sunny afternoon.

Makes Four Servings

2 cups cooked wheat berries, cooled
1/4 pound snow peas
1 1/2 cup bean sprouts
1 large carrot
1 cucumber
1/2 cup water chestnuts (canned will do)
1/4 cup rice wine vinegar
2 tablespoons soy sauce
2 tablespoons sesame oil
1 tablespoon sugar

1 teaspoon Chinese chili sauce
1/2 teaspoon crushed Szechuan peppercorns
1/4 cup minced scallion, tops included
2 tablespoons minced cilantro (fresh coriander)
2 tablespoons finely minced fresh ginger
1 teaspoon grated or minced orange zest
1 garlic clove, finely minced

Put the wheat berries in a large serving bowl.

Bring four cups of water to a rapid boil in a medium-sized saucepan. Trim the snow peas and drop them into the boiling water. After about five seconds, they will turn bright green. Using a slotted spoon, transfer them immediately to a bowl of ice water. This will ensure their crisp greenness. When they have cooled, drain them and pat dry. Cut them into fine julienne, and add them to the wheat berries.

Rinse and drain the bean sprouts, and add them to the serving bowl.

Peel the carrot and slice it thinly on a sharp diagonal to make elongated ovals. Stack up the ovals, a few at a time, and cut them into fine julienne. Add the julienne to the salad.

Peel the cucumber, cut it in half lengthwise, and scoop out the seeds. Cut each half into long, very thin strips, then cut the strips crosswise to make julienne slices one inch long. Add them to the salad.

Slice the water chestnuts into one-inch-long julienne. Add them to the salad.

Toss the salad to combine all of the ingredients thoroughly.

In a small nonmetallic bowl, mix the vinegar, soy sauce, sesame oil, sugar, chili sauce, peppercorns, scallion, cilantro, ginger, orange zest, and garlic. Blend well with a whisk.

Spoon the dressing over the salad and toss thoroughly so that all of the delicious ingredients are lightly and evenly coated. Make this one ahead of time and chill it thoroughly, then serve at your leisure.

Each serving contains:

- FIBER: 3 GRAMS • CHOLESTEROL: 0 MILLIGRAMS
- FAT: 9 GRAMS • CALORIES: 353

Egyptian Eggplant Couscous on a Bedouin of Winter Vegetables

Tantalize your guests with the aromatic fragrance of Near Eastern spices wafting from your kitchen. Egyptian Eggplant Couscous on a Bedouin of Winter Vegetables recreates the exquisite cuisine of the Sahara Desert. Accompany it with a warm glass of spiced apple cider (alcohol is forbidden to the initiated) and a square of pistachio nut loaf drizzled with clover honey, and your friends will suddenly find themselves at the gates of Mecca.

Makes Six Servings

3 1/2 tablespoons olive oil
2 medium onions, coarsely chopped
2 large carrots
2 medium tomatoes, peeled and coarsely chopped
1/4 cup raisins
1/4 teaspoon ground ginger
1/4 teaspoon saffron
1/4 teaspoon ground cinnamon
1/4 teaspoon cayenne pepper
2 tablespoons sugar
salt and freshly ground black pepper to taste

4 cups chicken or vegetable stock
1 large eggplant
1/2 cup whole blanched almonds
4 zucchini
1 acorn or butternut squash
1 8-ounce can chickpeas, drained
1 1/2 cups water
2 tablespoons unsalted butter
1 1/2 cups quick-cooking couscous

In a large, heavy-bottomed pot, heat two tablespoons of the oil over medium-high heat. Add the onions and sauté for ten minutes.

Trim and clean the carrots. Cut them in half lengthwise, and then cut each half in half again. Add the carrots to the onions and sauté for one minute.

Add the tomatoes, raisins, ginger, saffron, cinnamon, cayenne, sugar, and salt and black pepper. Stir well to blend. Add the stock, bring it all to a boil, and lower the heat. Cover the pot and simmer for twenty minutes.

While the broth is simmering, preheat the broiler and prepare the eggplant.

Trim away the top and bottom of the eggplant and slice it into half-inch rounds. Brush both sides of each slice lightly with one tablespoon of the oil. Transfer the rounds of eggplant to a broiler pan and broil on one side only until the flesh is soft and just beginning to blacken, two to four minutes. Let the slices stand until they are cool enough to handle. Tear them into strips about half an inch wide. Set them aside.

Heat the remaining oil in a skillet over medium temperature. Add the almonds and toast until golden brown. Keep an eye on them: they cook quickly and burn easily. Drain the almonds on paper towels and set them aside.

Trim the zucchini. Cut them in half lengthwise and slice each half in half again.

Peel and seed the squash. Cut it into two-inch cubes.

To the pot of simmering broth, add the zucchini, squash, and chickpeas. Cook, uncovered, about twenty minutes, until all of the vegetables are tender.

In a small saucepan, heat the water and butter. Bring to a boil.

Put the couscous in a shallow baking dish. Pour the boiling butter-water over it and stir well. Cover the couscous with foil and let it stand for five minutes. Fluff the grains with a fork.

To compose the exotic Egyptian Eggplant Couscous on a Bedouin of Winter Vegetables, remove the tender vegetables from the broth with a slotted spoon, and place them on a warmed large platter. Top the vegetables with a fluffy mound of couscous. Crown the couscous with strips of eggplant and whole almonds.

Ladle a cupful of the remaining broth into a small bowl. Pass the hot, peppery broth separately to moisten each serving to perfection.

Lean Grain Tip: Omit the butter and almonds.

Each Lean Grain serving contains:

- FIBER: 3.5 GRAMS • CHOLESTEROL: 0 MILLIGRAMS
- FAT: 11.8 GRAMS • CALORIES: 452

Cannelloni San Gimignano on Baked Tomatoes and Basil

The texture of bulgur is an inspired addition to everyone's favorite Italian pasta filling. The nutty flavor of the grain combines beautifully with the classic blend of ingredients — spinach, ricotta, and that dynamic duo, Parmesan and Romano. To soak up the mouth-watering baking juices, a large crusty baguette is a must. A lightly dressed arugula salad and goblets brimming with hearty Chianti will ensure the success of your dinner party. *Buon gusto.*

Makes Four Servings

1 pound fresh spinach
1/2 cup uncooked bulgur
1/2 cup water
8 ounces ricotta cheese
1 egg
1/4 cup plus 1 tablespoon grated Parmesan cheese
1/4 cup plus 1 tablespoon grated Romano cheese
1 teaspoon ground nutmeg
salt and freshly ground black pepper to taste
4 large ripe tomatoes
24 fresh basil leaves

6 tablespoons olive oil

1 lemon

1/4 teaspoon salt

1 large garlic clove

2 12-inch-square sheets fresh egg pasta dough

Wash the spinach to remove all traces of grit. Steam the spinach in a large pot with only the water that clings to the leaves. Cook, covered, over medium heat until the leaves are wilted, about three minutes. Drain the spinach, let it cool, then squeeze it dry with your hands and chop it finely.

In a small saucepan, bring the water to a boil. Add the bulgur. Remove the saucepan from the heat and cover it. Stirring occasionally, let the bulgur stand until all of the water is absorbed, about five minutes.

In a medium-sized bowl, combine the spinach with the bulgur, ricotta, egg, quarter cup of Parmesan, quarter cup of Romano, nutmeg, and salt and pepper. Mix well. Set this filling aside to let the flavors combine.

Cut the tomatoes into inch-thick slices. Large tomatoes will yield about four slices each.

Oil the bottom of a nine-by-nine-inch baking dish with one tablespoon of the oil. Arrange the tomato slices in a single layer, and top each round with two basil leaves. Drizzle on two tablespoons of oil. Set the baking dish aside.

Halve the lemon and squeeze the juice into a small glass bowl. Add the remaining oil and the quarter teaspoon of salt, and press in the garlic. Whip with a fork and set the lemon sauce aside.

Preheat the oven to 350 degrees.

Cut the pasta sheets into 12 six-inch squares and begin

to assemble the cannelloni. Lay out the pasta squares on a flat surface. Spread a heaping tablespoon of spinach filling down the center of each square, until you have used up all the filling. Roll the square pasta sheets into tubes, and place each cannellone, folded side down, on top of the tomatoes and basil leaves in the baking dish. Spoon the lemon sauce evenly over the cannelloni. Sprinkle with the remaining Parmesan and Romano.

Cover the dish with foil and bake for twenty to thirty minutes, or until the tomatoes begin to soften, releasing their own delicious juice to combine with the lemon sauce.

Remove the dish from the oven and let the cannelloni cool, uncovered, for several minutes. Serve each guest two cannelloni with stewed tomatoes and spoonfuls of the delicious baking juice over all. Don't forget the crusty bread for dunking!

Lean Grain Tip: Use part-skim ricotta in place of whole-milk ricotta. Replace the whole egg with two egg whites. Use eggless fresh pasta.

Each Lean Grain serving contains:

- FIBER: 2 GRAMS • CHOLESTEROL: 34 MILLIGRAMS
- FAT: 25 GRAMS • CALORIES: 576

Old World Tabletop Polenta Puttanesca

The presentation is La Scala, but the warmth of this pungent dish comes straight from the old world kitchens of the Italian countryside. Generations of Italian cooks have poured gleaming, golden polenta out of the pot and directly onto the tablecloth. The puttanesca sauce, with its vibrant flavor, is spooned over the polenta like the fiery crown of Mount Etna. Serve the Polenta Puttanesca with a bitter Italian endive salad and a platter of thinly sliced provolone cheese, prosciutto, and dry salami. And don't forget the hearty Sicilian red wine that will have your guests singing arias before the meal is through.

Makes Six Servings

3 tablespoons extra-virgin olive oil
1 2-ounce can anchovy fillets, drained
4 garlic cloves, crushed
1 35-ounce can Italian plum tomatoes, undrained
1 jar capers, drained (2 1/2 ounces)
1 1/2 cups imported black olives, pitted and chopped
freshly ground black pepper to taste
2 cups coarse yellow cornmeal (polenta)

1 tablespoon salt

7 to 8 cups cold water

Heat the oil in a medium saucepan over low heat. Add the anchovy fillets and garlic, and mash thoroughly with the back of a wooden spoon to form a smooth paste. Add the tomatoes with their liquid, capers, and olives. Mix well. Simmer the puttanesca sauce, uncovered, for one hour, stirring occasionally. Season with pepper. If the sauce is done before you have finished cooking the polenta, pour it into a ceramic serving bowl and keep it warm until you are ready to serve.

While the sauce is simmering, combine the cornmeal, salt, and seven cups of cold water in a large, heavy-bottomed saucepan. Cook the polenta for thirty minutes over low heat, stirring frequently with a polenta stick or large wooden spoon. (If the polenta becomes stiff, slowly add more water. Taste and add more salt if necessary.) A crust will begin to form on the sides and bottom of the saucepan. It is on the crust, rather than on the pan bottom, that the polenta now cooks. The polenta should be quite thick, but add more water if it becomes too difficult to stir.

Ten minutes before you are ready to serve, turn the heat to high and stir continuously. The polenta will develop a glistening sheen.

Meanwhile, seat your guests. Place a large cutting board in the center of the dining table and drape it with a large, clean white cloth or dish towel. As your guests watch, pour the shining, hot polenta onto the cloth with a back-and-forth motion. It will spread out somewhat.

Now comes the best part. Bring a polenta paddle or a large flat knife to pass around the table, and show your guests how to help themselves: hold the edge of the cloth nearest to you taut in one hand, and scrape the polenta with a flourish onto the paddle, then quickly onto a plate. The less adventurous can ladle the polenta from the pot onto warmed rustic plates.

Pass the bowl of puttanesca sauce, family style, for your guests to spoon on top of the polenta. Also pass the platter of cheese and meats.

Each serving contains:
- FIBER: .5 GRAMS • CHOLESTEROL: 4 MILLIGRAMS
- FAT: 10 GRAMS • CALORIES: 162

Thanksgiving Stuffed Cabbage with Cranberry Compote

This year perk up your traditional holiday table with Thanksgiving Stuffed Cabbage — a creative and lively autumn entree. Complement the occasion with such harvest savors as golden pumpkin soup, roasted potatoes with rosemary, and bright red Cranberry Compote. If you decide to offer pecan pie for dessert, your guests will be happily stuffed themselves.

Makes Six Servings

1 8-inch white cabbage
3 tablespoons peanut oil
2 medium onions, diced
1 celery stalk, diced
1 carrot, peeled and diced
4 ounces mushrooms, minced
1 cup cooked basmati rice, cooled
1 cup cooked wheat berries, cooled
1 apple, cored and diced
1/4 cup chopped walnuts
1/2 teaspoon dried sage
1/2 teaspoon dried thyme
salt and freshly ground black pepper to taste
1 egg, lightly beaten

2 cups chicken or vegetable stock
2 bay leaves
Cranberry Compote (recipe follows)

Bring a large pot of water to a boil. Core the head of cabbage and boil it until the outer leaves begin to loosen, about seven minutes. Using two long-handled spoons, remove the tender leaves from the outside of the cabbage, drain them on paper towels, and let cool to room temperature. Repeat this process until all of the cabbage leaves are tender, drained, and cooled, about twenty minutes in all.

Heat two tablespoons of the oil in a large frying pan over medium heat. Add half a cup of the diced onion and sauté for four minutes. Stir in the celery and carrot, and sauté for two minutes longer. Stir in the mushrooms and cook for another minute or two.

Put the sautéed vegetables in a large mixing bowl. Add

the rice and wheat berries, then the apple, walnuts, sage, thyme, and salt and pepper. Fold in the beaten egg and mix well to combine. Use your hands to roll the stuffing into twelve cylindrical portions.

On a clean work surface, arrange one large cabbage leaf, or several small leaves overlapping, with the cupped side up. Put a portion of stuffing in the center of the cabbage cup. Tuck and turn both ends up to cover the stuffing. Roll the leaf into a sausage shape to enclose the filling completely. Do not wrap too tightly, since the stuffing will expand a bit as it cooks.

Wipe out the frying pan. Add the remaining oil and heat to a moderate temperature. Add the remaining diced onion and sauté for about five minutes, or until limp and translucent. Arrange the stuffed cabbage rolls seam side down in a single layer on the bed of sautéed onions. Lightly sprinkle the tops with salt and pepper. Pour the stock over them and add the bay leaves. Heat the stock to a simmer. Cover the frying pan and continue to cook slowly, basting occasionally, until the stuffed cabbage is tender, about thirty minutes.

To serve the succulent Thanksgiving Stuffed Cabbage, spoon the sautéed onions over a large serving platter to create a delicious bed of flavor for the stuffed cabbage nestled on top. The Cranberry Compote should be served family style, passed hand-to-hand among your friends and loved ones in the time-honored spirit of the day.

Lean Grain Tip: Use two egg whites in place of the whole egg.

Each Lean Grain serving contains:

> • FIBER: 2 GRAMS • CHOLESTEROL: 0 MILLIGRAMS
> • FAT: 11 GRAMS • CALORIES: 259

Cranberry Compote

This shining, ruby-red condiment should be made at least one day ahead to permit the cranberries to soak up the zesty-sweet juice. Serve gently reheated or chilled, as you prefer.

Makes 1 1/2 Cups

1 cup water
1 cup dry white wine
1/2 cup sugar
1 lemon
1 tablespoon pure vanilla extract
12 ounces fresh cranberries

Heat the water, wine, and sugar to a simmer in a medium-sized saucepan.

Grate the lemon zest and add it to the saucepan. Squeeze the juice from the lemon and add it, along with the vanilla. Remove the saucepan from the heat and stir to dissolve the sugar completely.

Add the cranberries to the saucepan. The syrupy liquid should cover the berries by half an inch. Add more water if necessary. Reheat the syrup to barely simmering. Continue to cook until all the berries are tender, about twelve to fifteen minutes.

Remove the pan from the heat and let cool to room temperature for about thirty minutes. Put the compote in a covered nonmetallic bowl and refrigerate overnight.

When you are ready to serve, remove the cranberries from the poaching syrup with a slotted spoon and discard the liquid.

Prissy's Rice Puppies with Spiced Lentils and Cantaloupe Relish

Tangy with citrus and subtly spiked with ginger and a dash of Tabasco, Prissy's Rice Puppies with Spiced Lentils and Cantaloupe Relish will be the highlight of your own Twelve Oaks party. Set your table with frosted mint juleps or tart homemade lemonade and dainty bowls of Georgia peach ice cream pierced with wedges of shortbread, and your guests will be caught up in the spell of the Old South. Rest assured Scarlett O'Hara would have relished this piquant offering.

Makes Twelve Rice Puppies (Serves Four)

2 cups cooked white rice, cooled
2 eggs, lightly beaten
2 tablespoons all-purpose flour
2 scallions, minced, tops included
1 tablespoon grated lemon zest
1 tablespoon grated orange zest
1/2 teaspoon dried mustard
1 tablespoon fresh lemon juice
2 teaspoons Worcestershire sauce
1/4 teaspoon grated fresh ginger
dash of Tabasco sauce

salt and freshly ground black pepper to taste
2 tablespoons extra-virgin olive oil
mint sprigs and lemon wedges, for garnish
Spiced Lentils and Cantaloupe Relish (recipe
  follows)

Preheat the oven to 225 degrees.

In a medium bowl, combine the rice, eggs, and flour. Mix well to blend. Stir in the scallions, followed by the lemon and orange zest, mustard, lemon juice, Worcestershire sauce, ginger, Tabasco, and salt and pepper. Mix the batter thoroughly to combine all the ingredients.

In a large nonstick skillet, heat the oil over medium-high heat. When the oil is hot, drop in rounded tablespoons of the batter. Be careful not to crowd the skillet, as the rice puppies will spread to about three inches wide as they cook. Fry them until golden brown and crisp on the bottom, about four minutes. Turn them over and cook the other side for another two minutes. Remove the batch from the skillet, drain on paper towels, and keep hot in the oven. Repeat until you have used all the batter.

Present Prissy's Rice Puppies stacked high and adorned with mint sprigs and wedges of juicy lemon. Encourage your guests to help themselves to a dollop of the Spiced Lentils and Cantaloupe Relish.

Lean Grain Tip: Use three egg whites in place of the two whole eggs.

Each Lean Grain serving contains:

- FIBER: .5 GRAMS • CHOLESTEROL: 0 MILLIGRAMS
- FAT: 7.6 GRAMS • CALORIES: 152

Spiced Lentils and Cantaloupe Relish

You should prepare this exotic relish several hours in advance to allow the ingredients to marinate and blend for full flavor.

Makes 1 1/2 Cups

1/2 ripe cantaloupe, cut into 1/4-inch cubes
1/2 cup cooked lentils, drained
1/4 cup minced red bell pepper
1 scallion, minced, top included
1 tablespoon minced fresh parsley
1 tablespoon fresh lemon juice
salt and cayenne pepper to taste

Combine all the ingredients in a medium-sized bowl. Mix well, but gently. Serve at room temperature.

GRAIN INDEX

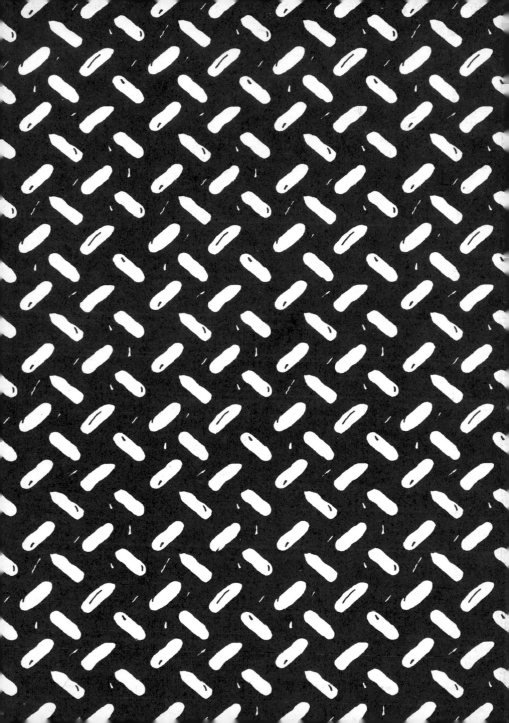